SUNDAY SERENADE

VOLUME II

Sammy Kaye's

SUNDAY SERENADE

VOLUME II

Book of Poetry

Copyright 1947

SERENADE PUBLISHING, INC.

First Printing 1947

Poetry is so akin to music.

In its diminuendos or crescendos of words,

It soothes or excites,

Leaving one calm or trembling;

But forever . . . remembering.

SAMMY KAYE

This book is sincerely dedicated
to the listeners and friends
of our Sunday Serenade.

FOREWORD

THE VERSES in this book comprise three groups: First and foremost, those chosen from our National Poetry Contest; second, those we have gathered in our travels throughout the country; third, selections from the world's poetic masterpieces.

The poems collected from our National Poetry Contest represent seven months of careful reading, grading, and selecting from many thousand entries. To all who competed, my sincere thanks. To those whose works the judges selected for this volume, my enthusiastic congratulations. Last, but not least, my heartfelt gratitude to the editors and to the judges: Kate Smith, Ted Malone, and Vernon Pope, for successfully completing a most difficult task.

You will recall many of the authors in the second group as old friends of the first book of Sunday Serenade poems; others are new contributors. I am sure you will join me in welcoming all of these.

The poems chosen from the treasury of world classics were included on the recommendation of our Sunday Serenade listeners. They have been requested many times and we are happy to include them in this collection.

This book represents a broad cross section of the poetic field, running the gamut from a simple idea, represented in poetic prose, on up to the more heroic complexities of the Shakespearian sonnet.

Here, then, are words — singing words — played by the minstrels of poesy on the heartstrings of the world. I hope your enjoyment of them will equal our pleasure in presenting them to you.

SAMMY KAYE
May 11, 1947

CONTENTS

N A T U R E

As a fond mother, when the day is o'er,
Leads by the hand her little child to bed,
Half willing, half reluctant to be led,
And leaves his broken playthings on the floor,
Still gazing at them through the open door,
Nor wholly reassured and comforted
By promises of others in their stead,
Which, though more splendid, may not please him more;
So Nature deals with us, and takes away
Our playthings one by one, and by the hand
Leads us to rest so gently, that we go
Scarce knowing if we wish to go or stay,
Being too full of sleep to understand
How far the unknown transcends the what we know.

HENRY WADSWORTH LONGFELLOW

HOW MUCH DO I LOVE YOU, DARLING?

How much do I love you, darling?
How can I answer this?
Can we measure the sweetness and passion
Of a lover's kiss?

Can we measure the dewy beauty
Of a fragrant summer rose,
Or the raindrops in the ocean—
And the depths of its repose?

Can we capture the song of the nightingale,
Or the moonbeam's silver light?
Can we capture the mystic wonder
Of a cloudless, windswept night?

Can we measure the length of laughter,
Or the sorrow when we part?
Can we define the anguish
Of another's broken heart?

How much do I love you, darling?
The volume, I must confess,
Cannot be found in earth or heaven—
My love is . . . measureless.

VALERIE JANE HIMMELHEBER

SPRING SUNSHINE

Spring has come, and I remember
How you found your way into my life.
You came to me the way spring sunshine
Comes stealing through an open window;
Softly, yet swiftly, and without warning—
Casting your golden light into
The slumbering chambers of my heart.
You quickly kindled there a fire
No power on earth could hope to stifle.
You came like sunlight, bursting through clouds,
Thawing the dismal cold within me.
You came to me like gentle rain,
Falling upon the thirsty earth,
And filling me with renewed desire.
Yet—I'm humbled before your shadow
And I ask no more of life than this . . .
That I may spend the rest of my days
With you . . .

GEORGE GINGELL

HEART'S PILGRIMAGE

A springtime valley once was mine—
    How soft the breeze! How fresh and fair
The flowers that grew about my feet!
    (Beloved, I found you there.)

And I have known the mountain's peak,
    With wind forever blowing south,
With stars above—(and very near
    The night I kissed your mouth.)

Across the desert of the years
    I see a path my feet must trace . . .
I scorn to carry bread and wine
    Or seek respite in any place.
(My only sustenance shall be
    The memory of your face.)

B. Y. WILLIAMS

SONNET

Shall I compare thee to a summer's day? . . .
Thou art more lovely and more temperate;
Rough winds do shake the darling buds of May,
And summer's lease hath all too short a date;
Sometimes too hot the eye of heaven shines,
And often is his gold complexion dimmed;
And every fair from fair sometime declines,
By chance, or nature's changing course, untrimmed.
But thy eternal summer shall not fade,
Nor lose possession of that fair thou owest,
Nor shall Death brag thou wanderest in his shade,
When in eternal lines to time thou growest.
    So long as men can breathe, or eyes can see,
    So long lives this, and this gives life to thee.

WILLIAM SHAKESPEARE

OUR LOVE

When the shadows of evening have lengthened,
And the fire in our hearts is aglow;
When my peace with the world has been strengthened;
It is then, dear heart, I know.

When the cares of the day are receding
And we watch as the flames ebb and flow,
Or we quietly glance from our reading,
It is then, dear heart, I know.

It's a love that belies all expression,
It's a richness that comes with the years,
It's the essence of life—it's depression—
It's laughter—it's work—and some tears.

My darling, it's everyday living
Made precious by you at my side,
And your life, so devoted to giving,
And your home, you have molded with pride.

When the shadows of evening have lengthened,
And the fire in our hearts is aglow;
Though my voice may be still, yet I'm strengthened
By your love, dear heart, I know.

PAULA DUKE SCHNEIDER

I CAN'T FORGET

There were other loves before you came,
And I may sometimes wish that we had never met;
But life without you could not be the same,
For having loved you once, I can't forget.

I always will remember how you smile,
How laughter lights a flame within your eyes.
So even though you lingered but a while,
I will recall a love born in the skies.

I will remember golden hours with tears,
The tenderness of hands that touched my own.
Though you may not be with me through the years,
With memories of you I'm not alone.

Yes, there were other loves before you came,
But I knew that first moment, when we met,
That life without you could not be the same,
For having loved you once, I can't forget!

BETIMA MACK

EVENING'S SOLITUDE

Your love comes to me on wings of velvet night.
Enchanted thoughts endow with gentleness and peace
The exalted spirit that now engulfs my very being.
My heart is yours, my soul in its entirety
Is yours. For you are the one I love. You are the love
That is the complete fulfillment of all my deepest desires.
You are the love that makes tomorrow live for me;
And though you are far from my side, I do not feel alone.
All through the dark monotony of the sunless hours,
I am caressed in the arms of night; arms that thrill me with
The touch that brings the memory of your arms about me,
Of your kiss upon my lips, of every moment we have shared.
The evening's solitude comforts me, and the serenade
Of the sighing wind through trees lends a haunting refrain
        to our love.
I feel your presence and I know we are one, and I send my love
To you on the wings of night. These are the messengers
That unite my soul with yours in eternal happiness.

VERA MARIE FRANZ

I WISHED FOR YOU

Did you see the first star last night, darling?
         I wished on it.
In the soft gray twilight, I stood alone,
         Thinking of you.
And, suddenly, out of the gathering dusk
         The star broke through.
So, with my love and faith in you, darling,
         I wished on it.

Fancy went astray; forgive me, dearest,
         But I wished for you,
Loving you so, and knowing it was wrong.
         How my heart sighed,
Though I understood that I must forget.
         You see, when I tried
To forget, I couldn't. So, forgive me, dear heart,
         I wished for you.

                                        JEAN WELBORN

INTRODUCTION

Thank you for being the one to introduce me to love.
You led me to walk in the sun,
To laugh and love and know happiness.
Your nearness became something dear to me,
Something warm and sweet,
Like the balminess of summer.
And then I knew that I wanted you near me always.
The first breath of love was like a clean, swift wind,
And I stood there, while my body thrilled to the feel of it.
Then, as summer deepened, and came the restless winds of autumn,
I saw new horizons in your eyes,
And I watched you go. But the love I had sworn
Stays in my heart and makes me long for you
When I hear the rain, and see familiar places,
And catch fragments of old songs that sigh of you.
Then my soul weeps for you.
But thank you, darling, for every memory—
Wonderful and bittersweet;
Above all, thank you for being the one I'll always love.

EILEEN HARDY

OL' DAN'L

The old man's eyes moved to and fro,
His cotton head was bending low.
So close to death—
With one last breath
He told me he feared not to go—away.

His story penetrated me;
And, as he lay in misery,
I listened to
His whole life through,
And almost shuddered inwardly—that night.

His haunting tone of truth so bold
Became as vivid as the cold;
He led a life
So full of strife
That now I saw my faults unfold—before me.

For I had done this old man wrong;
His grinding life had been no song;
And I had sinned
While he had grinned,
For he was good as time is long—forever.

His dying breath came just as he
Said, "Massa, will you pray for me?"
And with that word
A sigh was heard
And Dan'l died—so quietly—at sunrise.

The tears were streaming down my face;
I'd been so conscious of his race
I didn't give
Him chance to live;
Oh, God, please help me to erase—my sin.

His funeral was a small affair,
And negro spirituals filled the air.
On upturned sod
I swore to God
To have good faith and learn to care . . . Amen!

SHIRLEY SHERMAN

DID YOU FORGET SO EASILY

Did you forget, so easily,
    Those hours of perfect bliss?
Don't you remember how we thrilled
    To each soft touch and kiss?

Have you forgotten all of our
    Delightful plans and schemes?
Don't tell me they live, only now
    In my most cherished dreams.

Remember when you whispered those
    Sweet love words in my ear;
And vowed, between the kisses, that
    None else could be so dear?

Did parting tears drown memories
    Of hours shared breezily?
You didn't write. Dear one, did you
    Forget so easily?

LYLA MYERS

OLD LOVE

Don't tell me that I must not dream of old love;
For I will, as long as there are stars that stand so still—
Those stars that are remote as things I dream about,
But always there when candles of the day go out.

I dream of grass that's wet with lustrous pearls of dew
That glistened like the dreams we talked about.
And you were small and trembling as the leaves of trees
That breathed their fragrance all about us.

I think if God would take the stars down out of heaven,
And never let the lilacs bloom again,
Nor ever wet the grass with silvered dew drops
. . . I think perhaps I could forget you only then.

ADA McCLURG RUCKER

POSTPONEMENT

I love you with more tenderness
    Than I found easy words to say;
I meant to let you know—ah, yes—
    Some perfect time, some perfect way.
Still I remained expressionless,
    Deciding always, "not today."

Ah, useless that in grief I bow,
    And speak the words that were too slow!
Vain the caresses that somehow
    I waited too long to bestow.
What matter all my loving now,
    When you, beloved, cannot know!

B. Y. WILLIAMS

SONNET FROM THE PORTUGESE

If you must love me, let it be for naught
Except for love's sake only. Do not say,
"I love her for her smile—her look—her way
Of speaking gently—for a trick of thought
That falls in well with mine and surely brought
A sense of pleasant ease on such a day"—
For these things in themselves, beloved, may
Be changed, or change for thee—and love, so wrought
May be unwrought so. Neither love me for
Thine own dear pity's wiping my cheeks dry—
A creature might forget to weep, who bore
Your comfort long, and lose your love thereby!
But love me for love's sake, that evermore
You may love on, through love's eternity.

ELIZABETH BARRETT BROWNING

I STILL LOVE YOU

How can I forget what we thought was just a harmless flirtation?
That quick moment, when a glance made the sky
Seem like a million suns were shining;
That over-the-shoulder look;
That little hesitation, that comes before a glimpse of gladness.
In less than a heartbeat, we were holding hands,
And in less time than that, we knew it was love.
Yes, I'd been in love before, and like any other sentimental guy,
I was in love with love . . .
Who hasn't been?
But when you came along, everything stood still;
There was no one could have told me this wasn't love.
And as time went by, there was nothing I overlooked
To prove I loved you.
I must give you credit, though—
You played your part magnificently;
And you made me the greatest fall guy since Adam.
You used every trick in the book
And a few new ones you dreamed up just for the occasion . . .
All rolled up into one little game played with a heart—my heart.
I had to tell you all these things, because they're deep inside of me.
The only thing left for me to say is that I still love you . . .
And I always will.

SUNNY SKYLAR
DICK ROGERS

LOVE'S UNREASON

Love me not for comely grace,
For pleasing eye or face,
Nor for any outward part;
Not even for a constant heart.

For these may fail or turn to ill:
So you and I must sever.
Keep, therefore, a true woman's eye,
And love me still—but know not why!
Then you will have the same reason still
To dote upon me ever.

ANONYMOUS

LITTLE THINGS

I remember little things that made our
    Love so fine;
The smiling eyes and full red lips
    That sang and laughed with mine . . .
The quiet way you walked with me,
    Softly through our dreams . . .
The golden spectre of your hair
    In wistful moonlit streams . . .
The reassuring words you spoke,
    Soft kindness in your voice . . .
The way you liked to muss my hair . . .
    And laughingly rejoice.

These little things, all part of you,
    Are part of me, it seems,
For when I close my eyes and sleep
    You walk with me in dreams.

WILLIAM M. WALL

LOVE'S BENEDICTION

Your love is like a prayer that blesses me
And warms my heart with strange, new tenderness;
For I, who knew but storm and lightning thrust,
Could only grope and could but dimly guess
There would be shelter some day from the wind
That had blown out my one small lamp of trust;
How could I dream there would be bread and wine
When I had known only a beggar's crust?

Yet I, who doubted once, this truth have learned—
And it was you who taught my soul its creed—
As long as there is faith for each dark night,
There will be sustenance for each day's need.
And though we walk together or apart,
Whatever life may bring, I still shall be
Secure, content, and comforted to know
Your love is like a prayer that blesses me.

FRANCES BRANDON NEIGHBOURS

WHITE MOMENT

The day is long remembered, and the hour,
When you and I clasped hands as friend to friend—
Not knowing then that love's exquisite flower
Would blossom in our hearts until the end.
How casually and quietly we spoke,
That gray December twilight as we met;
But in your heart and mine a song awoke
A dream that you and I will not forget.
We did not need the halo of a moon
To crown that still, white moment—yours and mine—
Nor wish for music, while the wind's low tune
Played softly on the harps of swaying pine.
A heart grows sad that never holds a dream,
And roads are drab where love has never waited;
But those who see another's candle gleam
And light their own, in answer, are star-fated.
Swift years have passed . . but you and I remember
A snow-clad twilight etched on gray December.

MATTIE RICHARDS TYLER

BUILD A WALL

Build a wall of kindness
Around some lonely heart today.
Be a friendly guiding light
To a soul that's gone astray.

Build a wall of charity
And share with those who need.
In the book of life's recorded
Each good and noble deed.

Build a wall of happiness,
Shelter those you love.
Store this earthly treasure
In God's warehouse above.

Build a wall of character,
Bind each stone with prayer.
Let your thoughts of others be
When good fellowship you share.

Build a wall of things worth while.
Remember fellow-men, birds and trees.
In the counting of eternity,
None counts as much as these.

HERBERT TOWNSEND

NO GREATER FAITH

I have not earned the faith you have in me,
And yet I need you, as a child who wakes
Alone and frightened in the dark, to see
A phantom his own trembling shadow makes.
Your courage is a candle in the night,
Unwavering, while the winds of darkness blow
My dreams, like drifting smoke rings, out of sight
To that oblivion where my day dreams go.
When I have troubled thoughts, I turn to you;
When I would run from life, you bid me stand
To meet it, unafraid, as though we two,
With faith, could move a mountain hand in hand.
Life has no power to bend me to its will
When you know all my faults, and love me still.

RUTH M. THURMAN

I MAY FORGET

I may, in years to come, try
    vainly to recall
Just how, and when, and where we met—
    In summer or in fall.
I may forget the way you smile
    And wrinkle up your nose,
The color of your hair, your walk—
    I may forget all those!

Perhaps I will forget your voice,
    The starlight in your eyes.
And I may find with passing years
    This longing for you dies;
For as I try to weave a dream
    From words that we have said,
I will find that time has stolen
    All of memory's thread.

But, oh, my dear, when that day comes,
    I will not need your smile—
I will not long to hold you—hold
    You near to me the while.
It will not matter that years
    Ago we met. For only
After I have ceased to live
    Will I forget!

RUTH SALMON

THE BEGGAR

A rich woman gave me pearls—and a scornful look.
I didn't want her pearls; I flung them in the brook.
A man with eyes like polished stones offered me work,
And, in a year, a bounty promised—if I didn't shirk.

A gambler gave me money, but his eyes would not meet mine.
A workman tossed a coin for luck; in the dust I left it shine.
A housewife gave me food, and shooed me from her door.
A small boy ate an apple, and threw to me the core.

A cripple opened wide his door, and led me to his board;
We broke dry bread and drank strong tea from his small hoard.
He told a joke, we laughed together; my journey knew its end;
For here, at last, was all I'd asked . . . someone to call
    a friend.

Frances Ison Smith

LONGING

I looked for you last night in all the small
And quiet streets we knew. Inside the bare
And empty world, I sought your voice . . . and all
I found was loneliness. You were not there.
I listened for your laugh. There was no sound.
I hunted down your echo in the park;
The silence must have laughed . . . for all I found
Was pain and speechless shadows in the dark.

I called the shadows, asking for your name.
Again I heard the silent, speechless night.
I asked for words, but only echoes came.
I found just darkness when I'd looked for light.

I looked for you last night. I missed you then.
I'll look tonight again . . . again . . . . again.

MARY DOLAN

IF I SHOULD LEAVE YOU

If it should be that I must go,
    Unwilling though I be to part—
These words I leave to gladden your sad heart . .
    Of all I knew, of all I know,
You were my only love, sweetheart;
      You were the reason for my destined chart.

And if, when gone, you think of me,
    Who joined an eager caravan,
Whose fare is life, for passage to a star . . .
    I'll not forget, as you shall see;
Across the way I'll find a span
      To reach you and to tell you from afar.

Sometime, should raindrops kiss your cheek,
    It shall be I, whose only way
To give a kiss to you was from the sky . . .
    Or if the leaves at evening speak,
Thankful that you have passed that day;
      The whisper which you hear . . . it shall be I.

JIMMIE STULL

DON'T QUIT

When things go wrong, as they sometimes will,
    When the road you're trudging is all up hill,
When the funds are low and the debts are high,
    And you want to smile, but you have to sigh;
When care is pressing you down a bit,
    Rest—if you must—but don't you quit.

Life is queer with its twists and turns,
    As everyone of us sometimes learns,
And many a failure turns about
    When he might have won had he stuck it out;
Don't you give up, though the pace seems slow—
    You might succeed with another blow.

Often the goal is nearer than
    It seems to a faint and faltering man,
Often the struggler has given up
    When he might have captured the victor's cup;
And he learned too late, when the night slipped down,
    How close he was to the golden crown.

Success is failure turned inside out—
    The silver tint of the clouds of doubt—
And you never can tell how close you are,
    It may be near when it seems afar;
So stick to the fight when you're hardest hit—
    It's when things seem worst that you musn't quit.

AUTHOR UNKNOWN

MY SON

Son . . . my little son, come close and listen to what
    I have to say.
Perhaps you'll find this a little hard to understand,
But I want to tell you about someone
Who is very close to my heart . . .
Someone who gave me everything that's fine in life
And made, of our life together, a thing of surpassing beauty.
Then, my son, you came along,
Bringing a new kind of happiness.
No matter how long or weary the days—and there were many—
She found time to love us both with every fibre of her being.
In you, son, I see all the things that made her dear to me:
A smile, so much like sun through trees;
A voice—soft, like the breath of a breeze;
And, son, when you walk into a room, I see her again,
Filling every darkened corner with sweetness and light.
These are the things I wanted you to know.
And so, goodnight, my son . . . just one thing more
Before you go to sleep; say one short prayer for her.
I know that she is near tonight because, you see,
This is our anniversary!

SAMMY KAYE
&
GEORGE GINGELL

IT SEEMS BUT YESTERDAY

It seems to me but yesterday you came into my life;
You brought along the sunshine and settled much of strife.
It seems to me but yesterday my eyes beheld your own,
And you were sweet and regal, like a queen upon a throne.

But even though the time has fled, just like a thousand years,
I've worshipped every blessed hour and shed a thousand tears.
I've cradled you close to my heart and every joy I've known.
I think by day and dream by night you are my very own.

And though the years may come and go throughout eternity,
I'll remember all the little things that mean so much to me.
The merry twinkle in your eyes, your lips, your brow divine;
The sweetness of your heart within, and all that's good and fine.

And when another thousand years have swiftly passed away,
I'll still remember all the joys that I have known today.
I'll still remember happy hours that I have spent with you,
And count them over one by one, so sweet, but yet too few.

NAT L. ROYSTER

MY STAR

As I look out from my window
   And see the stars at night,
I think they represent past friends
   Who, to my life, brought light.

The dim stars are for those who passed,
   So quickly, with a smile.
The bright ones typify dear friends
   I loved a long, long while.

As days pass fleetly by, I want
   To be the kind of friend
Who leaves delightful memories
   With all — until the end.

And if the stars perpetuate
   Your friends each lovely night,
Oh, may one bring a thought of me —
   And be extremely bright!

LYLA MYERS

HAD I LOVED YOU LESS

Had I loved you less, I could now weep
And ease my tragic burden in some part.
Had I loved you less, I could expose
This awful grief I carry in my heart.

Had I loved you less, I could cry out
And walk in tears with time, until at last
My waning protestations made me know
The highest tides of agony were past.

But my love for you went beyond words,
Defying all my efforts to express,
In any way, the measure of my cup.
My love was thus, my grief can not be less.

EDITH HUTCHINS SMITH

IN SEPTEMBER

I think, perhaps, I miss you most in September, when rain
Patters on crisp leaves and comes crying at the window.
I remember you so many Septembers ago —
The woody scent of your hair as you sat looking into
      a campfire;
The little yellow coat about your shoulders; the graceful
Curve of your lips in firelight.
I remember the small brown ring on your finger — the one
      we bargained
For from gypsies; leaves spinning at your feet on the way home;
The little dog who followed us.
I think, perhaps, I miss you most when leaves go blowing
      down the street;
Or when I see two people walking on a country road . . . .
      two people
Who might be us.
And when I listen, darling — closely — there is the
      almost undetectable
Sound of your footsteps, leaving their print to patter on
      my heart
. . . on and on . . . through forever.
Wherever you are, my dear, do you remember . . .
      in September?

BETTY JANE BALCH

BECAUSE IT IS NOVEMBER

Because it is November, I am remembering you,
The half forgotten evenings of preciousness we knew.

I am remembering apples, the little wooden bowls
Of popcorn, crisp and snowy, that we made over coals.

Because it is November, I see again the fire
Piled high with southern pinewood, I feel the sharp desire.

To speak of all the old things—the winter, and the days
That start with fragrant coffee, and end with twilight's haze.

I often wonder, darling, if you by chance still wear
The soft angora sweater, with all the silky hair.

And do your lips look lustrous and rose in candleglow?
And are there any new songs you think I ought to know?

Because it is November, I am remembering you;
It was a very special, and happy month we knew.

And although summer's moments are filled with ecstasy,
You and November, darling, are still a part of me.

BETTY JANE BALCH

TOMORROW

It's the blue-and-goldest morning that October ever brought.
All the upland's swept with scarlet where the maple flames
      have caught.
Purple mists roll up the valley, burning smoky in the sun,
And the lowland's laced with azure where the swollen
      waters run.
There's a tang that makes the blood race, and a beauty
      makes you ache,
And today is ours, my darling, though tomorrow hearts will
      break.

You are walking here beside me in the old, familiar way.
And we'll see no other hours past the golden ones today;
Just to touch you, feel you near me, sing the songs we
      love once more.
Ah, the sands are yellow glowing, there's a soft wind blows
      inshore
Where the long October noontime slants so warmly on the lake;
And today I will be happy, though tomorrow hearts may break.

FLORENCE B. JACOBS

WHEN YOU WENT AWAY

I could only watch you go—
Without a sign of feeling;
Nor with a single gesture show
My soul that bled from kneeling.
They must not see how my heart bowed
Against the slanting rain of tears
That welled within me, like a flood
Of longing, pain, and fears.
I could not take you in my arms,
Implore you not to go;
Nor taste the nectar from yours lips,
Or say, "I love you so!"
But you consoled me with your eyes—
The message they conveyed.
Although your lips were sealed, as mine,
You said, "Don't be afraid . . .
This is not—it cannot be—
The end for you and me!
The love we share will rise above
These moments and be free.
We'll meet again some distant day
Never to say goodbye.
But until then, remember, dear,
That love will never die.
Love cannot die for you and me,
Though it will have to wait
To be released for happiness
By something we call fate!"

MURIEL WILKERSON

45

TO YOU, DARLING

Darling . . .

Even though your every thought is of someone else,
And your every desire is for someone else,
I know that, in my empty loneliness,
You would not begrudge my thoughts of you.

Because I loved you so much,
My heart was groping for a tiny spark,
Hidden in some far, secret corner of your heart
So deep that even you did not realize
It existed.

Maybe someone else will bear my name,
But there is a part of my being that she
Will never own,
Because I have known the wonder of your kisses,
Gentle as spring rain.

Darling,
Today I say I will forget—that I will hate you;
But what's the use,
When I know that tomorrow
I will only love you more.

EVELYN B. MALONE

46

OF ALL THINGS BEAUTIFUL

You are part of all things beautiful . . .
Like the fragrance of delicate flowers
That bloom after warm spring showers;
Like great clouds that float on high
Across a pale blue summer sky.

You are part of all things beautiful . . .
Like the sound of the angelus ringing
And the voices of children singing;
Like the strains of organ music that swell
Above the toll of the chapel bell.

You are part of all things beautiful . . .
Like the moon, whose soft yellow light
Disperses the shadows of night;
Like the quiet peace of eventide
And the joy in having you by my side.

You are part of all things beautiful . . .
And you always will be,
For heaven has made you so.
Yet, above all things beautiful,
I treasure the love you gave to me.

WILLIAM THOMAS RAIDT

I MISS YOU

I miss you in the morning, dear,
    When all the world is new;
I know the day can bring no joy,
    Because it brings not you.
I miss the well-loved voice of you,
    Your tender smile for me,
The charm of you, the joy of your
    Unfailing sympathy.

I miss you at the noontime, dear;
    The crowded city street
Seems such a desert now, I walk
    In solitude complete.
I miss your step beside my own,
    The light touch of your hand,
The quick gleam in the eye of you—
    So sure to understand.

I miss you in the evening, dear,
    When daylight fades away;
I miss the sheltering arms of you
    To rest me from the day.
I try to think I see you yet,
    There where the firelight gleams—
Weary at last I sleep, and still
    I miss you in my dreams.

B. Y. WILLIAMS

SNOW REVERIE

It's wintertime again,
And mem'ries come rushing back
Like snowflakes scurrying past my window pane.
And, framed in my casement's frost encrusted lace,
I catch momentary glimpses of your face
As each white flurry dances wildly by.

On such a night as this,
Love's last lingering ember
Was kindled anew in the passion of a parting kiss.
I sit alone, watching and wondering, now,
If some wind-tossed flake will kiss your brow
And make you pause in recollection.

Are you remembering, too,
A winter ride across the trackless white?
I haven't forgotten, have you?
We rode earthbound, yet immune to time's swift flight;
Afraid to even breathe our heart's delight
Lest we shatter the spell of that immortal moment.

Undying love we promised,
While all the silent stars looked down
In muted admiration as we kissed.
That was, oh, so many snows ago.
Wherever you are, I wonder if you know
That an ember of our love is burning still.

GEORGE GINGELL

49

ROMANTIC SONNET

I cannot write of love when in my heart
December's bleakness holds its frigid sway;
When sorrow's doleful messengers impart
Their dismal dirge of loneliness. Today
Your bitter tears are all I know of love.
But if they prove light rains that prophesy
The promises of springtime, and if above
This clouded gloom shines a brighter, bluer sky;
If, from this barren seed should spring anew
The love long buried under winter's snows,
Then I should write such poetry for you,
Its beauty would supplant the darkest woes;
My eloquence would know no earthly bars,
For I would pluck a poem from the stars.

Dorothy Bagnall

PRAYER FOR A NEW YEAR

With the clamor and the tolling of the bells,
The old year, like a weary traveler, comes finally to his rest.
In trembling voice, he whispers with his dying breath
A last will and testament for the new year.
To children he bequeaths golden dreams and light hearts,
To youth, strength and wisdom.
To mothers, love and kindly care;
And to fathers, fortitude and faith.
To those who stand alone, he offers hope and friendship;
And to all mankind, the precious gift of understanding.
All these and more the passing year bequeaths;
They are ours for the taking.
Now, in that brief moment
Between the passing of the old and the coming of the new,
Let me resolve with all my strength
To use well my full measure of this rich heritage,
Keeping, always, the vision of man's humanity to man.
I pray that I may have the grace to go forward steadfastly,
That I may bring love and hope and charity to those in need,
That I may be intolerant of evil,
Yet ever ready to forgive the penitent.
And—one last prayer—that through the years to come
I may never lose the faith of those I love.

GEORGE GINGELL

PERSISTENCE

Let them say you have forgotten.
Let them shout I was a fool to care.
I'll have no weeping in remembrance
Of a dream so wondrous fair.

My moment was the radiance of your smile,
The precious thrill of warmth
That lingered while we were together.

My life was knowing you were there,
Feeling your gentle touch,
And, though these lovely things have fled,
How can they say our love is dead?

There is nothing to lament.
We met, and loved, and went
Our separate ways.
We spoke no words of sadness,
You and I.
No tears to mar the memory
Of our last goodbye;
No tears . . . no stifled sigh.

And so,
We follow our accustomed patterns,
My heart and I,
Certain that the sun
Another dawn will bring.
Certain and together
My heart and I,
Await the coming of spring.

Carol Abrahamson

LIVING

To touch the cup with eager lips and taste, not drain it;
To woo and tempt and court a bliss—and not attain it;
To fondle and caress a joy, yet hold it lightly,
Lest it become necessity and cling too tightly;
To watch the sun set in the west without regretting;
To hail its advent in the east—the night forgetting;
To smother care in happiness—discouraging sorrow;
To hold the present close—not questioning tomorrow;
To have enough to share—to know the joy of giving;
To thrill with all the sweets of life . . . is living.

AUTHOR UNKNOWN

"LISTEN, SON:"

"I am saying this to you as you lie asleep with one little paw crumpled under your cheek and the curls stickily wet on your plump forehead. I have stolen into your room alone. Just a few minutes ago, as I sat reading my paper in the library, a hot, stifling wave of remorse swept over me. I could not resist it. Guiltily I came to your bedside.

"These are the things I was thinking, son: I had been cross to you. I scolded you as you were dressing for school because you gave your face merely a dab with a towel. I took you to task for not cleaning your shoes. I called out angrily when I found you had thrown some of your things on the floor. At breakfast I found fault, too. You spilled things. You gulped down your food. You put your elbows on the table. You spread butter too thick on your bread. And as you started off to play and I made for my train, you turned and waved a little hand and called, 'Good-bye, Daddy,' and I frowned, and said in reply, 'Hold your shoulders back.'

"Then it began all over again in the later afternoon. As I came up the hill road I spied you down on your knees playing marbles. There were holes in your stockings. I humiliated you before your boy friends by making you march ahead of me back to the house. Stockings were expensive and if you had to buy them you would be more careful. Imagine that, son, from a father. It was such stupid, silly logic.

"Do you remember later when I was reading in the library, how you came in, softly, timidly, with a sort of hurt, hunted look in your eyes? When I glanced up over my paper, impatient at the interruption, you hesitated at the door. 'What is it you want?' I snapped. You said nothing, but ran across, in one tempestuous plunge; and threw your arms around my neck and kissed me again and again, and your small arms tightened with an affection that God had set blooming in your heart and which even neglect could not wither. And then you were gone, pattering up the stairs.

"Well, son, it was shortly afterwards that my paper slipped from my hands, and a terrible sickening fear came over me. Suddenly I saw myself as I really was. in all my horrible selfishness, and I felt sick at heart. What has habit been doing to me? The habit of complaining, of finding fault,

54

or reprimanding, all of these were my rewards to you for being a boy. It was not that I did not love you; it was that I expected so much of youth. I was measuring you by a yardstick of my own years.

"And there is so much that is good, and fine, and true in your character. You did not deserve my treatment of you, son. The little heart of you is as big as the dawn itself, over the wide hills. All this was shown by your spontaneous impulse to rush in and kiss me good-night. Nothing else matters tonight, son.

"This is a feeble atonement. I know you would not understand these things if I told them to you during your waking hours, yet I must say what I am saying. I must burn sacrificial fires, alone, here in your bedroom, and make free confession. And I have prayed God to strengthen me in my new resolve. Tomorrow I will be a real daddy. I will chum with you, and suffer when you suffer and laugh when you laugh. I will bite my tongue when impatient words come. I will keep saying as if it were a ritual: 'He is still a boy—a little boy.'

"I am afraid I have visualized you as a man. Yet as I see you now, son, crumpled and weary in your cot, I see that you are still a baby. Yesterday you were in your mother's arms, your head on her shoulder,—I have asked too much, too much.

"Dear Boy, Dear little son, a penitent kneels at your infant shrine, here in the moonlight. I kiss the little fingers and the damp forehead and the yellow curl. Tears come, and heartache and remorse, and also greater, deeper love, when you ran through the library door and wanted to kiss me. Goodnight, Sonny—from this hour on we're pals, you and dad."

AUTHOR UNKNOWN

55

DREAMS AND REALITIES

I dreamed of love . . . how it would come
And sweep me swiftly off my feet;
Would change my world, transforming it,
To make my happiness complete.

I dreamed of one whose smile would stir
A thrill of joy within my breast
And leave a song deep in my heart
That would dispel my soul's unrest.

I tried to fit my dreams into
Realities that came my way,
I told myself that this was it;
All I had dreamed of yesterday.

But had I known what I know now
Of disillusionment and pain,
I would have kept my dreams instead,
And realized my loss was gain.

SARA SANDT

THE LAND WHERE DREAMS
COME TRUE

I hope I may find it some day—
    The land where dreams come true;
Where clouds of doubt are blotted out
    And skies are always blue;
Where there is joy without alloy;
    Where faith and hope abound;
Where sighs and tears and griefs and fears
    Are nowhere to be found;
Where flowers bloom and sweet perfume
    Is wafted on the breeze;
Where all day long a red bird's song
    Comes lilting through the trees.

I hope that you may be there, too,
    Just waiting, dear, for me;
And that your love, like stars above,
    Will ever faithful be.
If you're not there, I shall not care
    To keep my rendezvous,
For all my dreams and plans and schemes
    Are centered, dear, on you.
But if you're near, I'll know no fear,
    Whatever may betide;
I'll sing a song, be brave and strong,
    If you are by my side.

And so, I pray, some happy day,
    We'll meet again, we two,
If fate is kind, we'll surely find
    The land where dreams come true!

EDITH S. NORRIS

I DREAMED LAST NIGHT

I dreamed last night . . .
And there, in the shadows of my quiet room,
You came to me and spoke my name.
You took my hands and looked deep into my eyes;
There were no words, no sound but the steady fall of rain.

We sat before the hearthfire, feeling its gentle warmth,
Just as we did before, in the same old place.
We laughed and chatted in the same old way,
You even teased me, just to make me blush.
And all the while our hearts cried out for time to stay.

Tonight, I'll dream again . . .
And even though you're far away,
My dreams will keep you ever near to me
Until some day you come back to stay.

VENA MOLLOY BURT

LINES TO A LOST LOVE

"Let's break up," you said to me, so casually.
How can I forget those burning words?
And I had prayed with all my heart that night
That all our little differences might end;
That you might see that I was all you'd ever desire;
That you would find me good and worthy of your love.
But all you said was "Let's break up!"
Is this the answer to my fervent prayer?
Could you—do you know you broke my heart?
Have you forgotten how, on so many nights, our hearts beat
In a kind of music that only two in love can make?
Has your memory lost the thrill of brief, stolen minutes
Of love that knew nothing but sheer ecstasy?
And now you say you can't love quite enough
To forget our silly little differences.
Oh, but I have love enough for both of us,
Enough to set my slowly breaking heart at ease
If you would show the slightest faith in me.
So, I shall faithfully pray each day for strength
To wait until your love comes back to me.

MARY E. DUGGAN

HOW, WHY, AND WHEN

How do I love you?
I love you with the peace of a warm blue sky;
With the fidelity of the pure white stars,
With the warmth of a blazing torch;
With the sorrow of a lonely pine
Silhouetted against a dead sky.
That is how I love you.

Why do I love you?
I love you for the way your eyes talk to me,
And for the feeling of happiness that
Overwhelms my heart when you touch me.
I love you for the music
That you give me in all things.
That is why I love you.

When do I love you?
I love you when I am full of joy;
When you are near to me;
When you are as far away as distant stars.
I love you when you spite me,
And even when I am forsaken.
That is when I love you.

I love you with all the strength and faith
Of a sturdy tree.
And I only wonder sometimes
How and why and when . . . do you love me?

NORMA LOUISE MARTIN

LOVING YOU

Loving you is like having within my reach
All that I shall ever want to hold, or touch, or know.
Loving you is like gentle rain in springtme,
Full of warmth and comfort.
Knowng your love brought new life
Into the darkened chambers of my heart.

Through your love, I knew for the first time
The beauty of a dream come true,
And the full meaning of contentment.
This love of ours came quietly,
Making its presence known as subtly
As the unfathomed silence after storm,
Or the dim-lit solitude of a holy place.

Loving you is strangely beautiful;
It is something beyond definition,
Beyond the power of mere words to express.
My love for you could have had no earthly beginning;
It will have no ending.
Loving you is finding the essence of eternity.

JOYCE W. WALL

A SONG AT EVENING

Now that the lamps are lighted in the sky,
    And in the windows, too,
I bid the day a last and fond good-bye,
    And think of you.

I pray that evening shadows, dear as these,
    Enfold you where you are;
And that your vision, through the darkness, sees
    This same gold star.

That all the clamor of your day is still,
    Even as mine is now;
That you have watched the moon behind the hill
    Which lifts its brow.

And that a peace descends upon our way,
    Unutterably bright . . .
Love, through the distance, can you hear me say,
    "Good-night! Good-night!"

CHARLES HANSON TOWNE

SOFTLY AS THE RAIN

Gently, softly as the rain
Falls in warm spring showers,
So may my love fall on your heart.
And with love's golden powers—
Just as surely as the rain
Brings out the summer flowers—
May my love, your dear heart claim;
Gently, softly as the rain.

FRANCES WEHLE

THE PSALM OF LIFE

Tell me not, in mournful numbers,
Life is but an empty dream!—
For the soul is dead that slumbers,
And things are not what they seem.

Life is real! Life is earnest!
And the grave is not its goal;
Dust thou art, to dust returnest,
Was not spoken of the soul.

Not enjoyment, and not sorrow,
Is our destined end or way;
But to act, that each tomorrow
Find us farther than today.

Art is long, and time is fleeting,
And our hearts, though stout and brave,
Still, like muffled drums, are beating
Funeral marches to the grave.

Lives of great men all remind us
We can make our lives sublime,
And, departing, leave behind us
Footprints in the sands of time.

Let us, then, be up and doing,
With a heart for any fate;
Still achieving, still pursuing,
Learn to labor, and to wait.

HENRY WADSWORTH LONGFELLOW